VOGUE

essentials

VOGUE
essentials

lingerie

Anna Cryer

contents

introduction

fashion's hidden agenda

→ In contrast to the work for
which he is perhaps better known
– posters for the Stanley Kubrick
films *A Clockwork Orange* (1971)
and *Full Metal Jacket* (1987) and
album covers including David
Bowie's *Aladdin Sane* (1973) –
illustrator Philip Castle wielded
his pen for the 1 March 1968 story
"Print for the Body Beautiful". His
artwork delineates lissom, boyish
figures with Marcel-waved hair and
references the garçonne look of
the Twenties. "New fundamental
fashion is flowing in a fluid line,
light and alive with little flower
prints, with spiralling splashes of
patterns. Quite naturally shaped
for summer, quite beautiful,"
commented *Vogue*. The matching
bras and panty girdles in nylon
and Lycra by Warner's, Berlei and
Lovable are described as "trim",
"spare" and "featherlight", and are
strewn with "summer blooms" and
"seed packet flowers".

"There is something altogether wrong and abnormal about the woman who is not frightfully keen about lingerie in general and her own in particular," opined *Vogue* in 1918. "For after all, lingerie is what comes nearest to a woman's heart and naturally it gives her more real and intimate satisfaction than any other part of her wardrobe. Nothing can equal the pleasant glow of knowing that one's 'undies' are absolutely and impeccably right."

It's the first thing we put on and the last we take off. It can support, cosset, restrain and reveal our bodies. The word "lingerie" (from *linge*, the French for "linen") conjures a frisson that "bras-and-pants" simply doesn't. Rather than practicality and comfort, it suggests romantic intent, seduction and secrecy. And just as the word has a certain potency, so the images of lingerie in *Vogue* over the past century or so offer more than just an overview of changing underwear fashions. They reflect ideas of propriety, fabric innovations and the ever-changing fashion silhouette, not to mention how the boundary between under- and outerwear has been blurred in recent years.

Underwear, as we know it today, originated in the 19th century. For the previous five hundred years, the boned corset, worn over a washable cotton or linen chemise, with nothing underneath it below the waist, had been the predominant undergarment for women. By the late Victorian era, when the corset had evolved to a particularly cruel S-bend shape, pushing out the bust and buttocks, there were growing concerns among health professionals about the brutal physical constraints to which the corset subjected

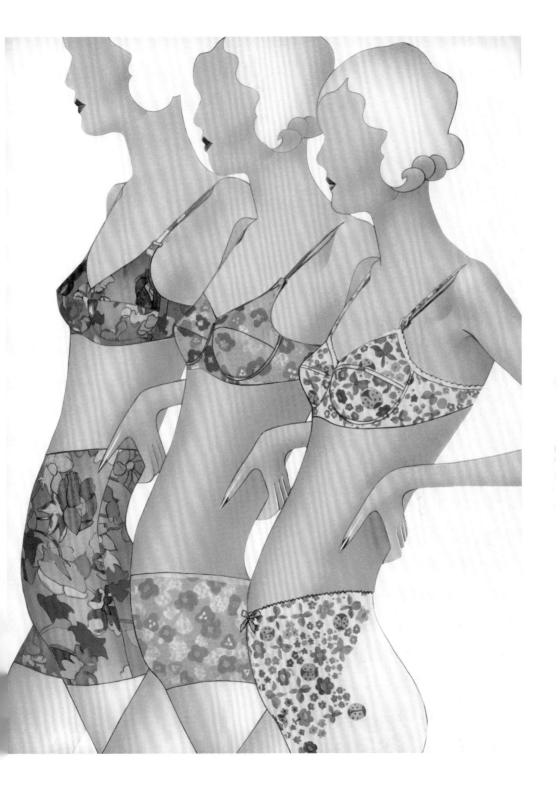

the body, and these chimed with the cause of The Rational Dress Society, which argued that "freedom" from corsetry was necessary if women were to play a greater role in society.

In 1906, fashion designer Paul Poiret declared an end to the corset with the launch of his new columnar silhouette, challenging the prevailing curvaceous Edwardian figure. Less a death knell, though, it proved more a spur to the corset's evolution, a division of the garment into two separate items. As the corset began to drop below the waist to concentrate on shaping the diaphragm and hips, it left the bust unsupported, thereby prompting the development of boned bodices – forerunners of the modern-day bra.

Social customs and morals relaxed in the optimism and prosperity brought on by the end of the Great War, and the Twenties was a decade of dramatic social and political change. Women achieved the right to vote and entered the workforce in record numbers. The fashion figure became straighter and more androgynous – the "garçonne" look, epitomized by film star Clara Bow, called for bobbed hair and a boyish figure. Shift-like "flapper" dresses barely acknowledged bust or hip, waistlines dropped and breast-flattening bandeau tops became popular. While this style was fine for those of slender build, it wasn't practical for everyone, and the corset, albeit slimmer in line than 15 years before, still provided much needed support for women with fuller figures.

There was plenty of lingerie coverage in *Vogue* in the Twenties and Thirties, with the magazine looking to Paris for the trends. Sometimes entire issues were devoted to it, perhaps not surprising given the exquisite fabrics, detail and colours used, and the fact that the term "lingerie" also embraced tea dresses, peignoirs and nightclothes, which together formed a woman's trousseau. Much of it was handmade, a sign of luxury and social status.

Structure gradually returned to the fashion silhouette in the Thirties and Forties. Elsa Schiaparelli pioneered padding for the shoulders, and the waistline settled back into its natural place. The influence of the movie industry reached Europe, and in an intercontinental cultural exchange, Madame Vionnet's bias-cut dresses from Paris (which continue to influence designers today) became the go-to evening wear for Hollywood screen sirens. Their figure-skimming fit necessitated smooth, bulk-free underpinnings, so girdle designs incorporated sleek elastic fabrics, such as rayon, rubber and elastic, and invisible zipper closures. The word "brassiere" was shortened to "bra" in the Thirties and

← In the story "Prima Donna" from September 2013, model Catherine McNeil fixes the viewer with a gimlet eye that feels as much a threat as an invitation. The fact that her face is veiled, her arms covered and her hands gloved serves to heighten the eroticism of her revealed cleavage. The beauty note in the caption amplifies the sexual overtone: "an intense, just bitten lip is the perfect adornment to a seductive lace veil". She wears a silk and lace bra by the Parisian designer Carine Gilson, who is renowned for her couture approach to lingerie and use of exquisite fabrics, such as Lyon silk and Chantilly lace.

VOGUE
DEC £3.30

Kylie:
Princess
of Pop

Sparkle

the garment's manufacture became a major industry. Fishnet stockings appeared and nylon hosiery debuted, quickly becoming all the rage.

World War II had a major impact on the style and manufacture of women's clothing. As women undertook a wider variety of jobs to assist with the military effort, the fashion silhouette developed a strong-shouldered, masculine look, and rationing, protection and material shortages informed the design of uniform and "utility" clothing. Sturdy woollen and cotton underpinnings prevailed over gossamer-fine silks and satins. Underwiring began to be used in bra construction. Military terminology even influenced product marketing: Maidenform designed the Chansonette bra, with its conical structure directing each breast upward and out from the torso, which became better known as the torpedo, or bullet, style. Actresses Lana Turner, Jayne Mansfield and Marilyn Monroe became known as "sweater girls" for the tight, figure-enhancing tops they wore over them.

Christian Dior's New Look in 1947 provided a post-war boost to underwear manufacturers, because the silhouette relied on specific undergarments to structure it. "Without foundations there can be no fashion", the designer proclaimed. The corsetry revival continued through the Fifties, in tune with the renewed emphasis on post-war domestic femininity, and the decade closed with the creation of the Barbie doll, echoing the large-chested, small-waisted ideal.

The Sixties, like the Twenties, saw enormous changes for women, with a new emphasis on youth, work, social freedoms and birth control. Fashion changed dramatically, eschewing the waist and becoming linear and short. In response, underwear began to diminish in size. Rudi Gernreich's lightweight, seamless, sheer "no-bra bra" was a revolutionary departure from the heavy, structured styles of the previous decade and heralded a move toward more natural shapes and softer fabrics. Sheer fabrics, prints and pattern were introduced, bras and knickers came in colourful matching sets, and tights meant suspenders and stockings could be dispensed with.

The women's liberation movement gathered momentum, despite no bras actually being burned, and the bra itself became a symbol of feminist activism when Germaine Greer referred to it in *The Female Eunuch* (1970) as "a hideous symbol of male oppression". As underwear was reduced to barely-there essentials

(and sometimes dispensed with altogether) in the hippie days of the Seventies, it provided less support for women wishing to conform to the contemporary ideal of the skinny body shape, so they began to turn to alternative measures such as dieting, physical exercise and cosmetic surgery.

The buffed, toned, fit body was the ideal in the Eighties. Jane Fonda made it cool to work out, and by the end of the decade Amazonian models were stalking the runways and the pages of *Vogue*. Fashion designers honoured the newly toned physique – Azzedine Alaïa's body-conscious dresses won him the nickname "king of cling", and Donna Karan endeared herself to legions of women by acknowledging the existence of hips and curves and introducing control underwear. Wolford's black opaque tights sheathed miniskirted legs. The corset re-emerged, championed by Vivienne Westwood, Jean Paul Gaultier, Christian Lacroix and Thierry Mugler, but rather than a means of constraint, it now became a symbol of feminine power.

Images in *Vogue* in 1992 of a waif-like Kate Moss in barely-there knickers were a counterpoint to the glossy hedonism of the Eighties and epitomized the new era of grunge and so-called "heroin-chic". Calvin Klein caught the zeitgeist with his-and-hers underwear ads featuring a topless Moss and Marky Mark (Mark Wahlberg), and established brand names on the waistband of underwear as a status symbol. Around the same time, model-turned-entrepreneur Elle Macpherson launched her Intimates lingerie line, the first (and one of the most successful) of many similar model ventures. Petite but full-breasted figures of female lifeguards on the television series *Baywatch* (1989–99) caught the nation's imagination, and in 1994 Eva Herzigova brought traffic to a standstill with her appearance in the cleavage-enhancing Wonderbra ads. It was amid these wildly varying tropes of female vulnerability and empowerment that lingerie began to cross the line from secret to public.

The phrase "underwear as outerwear" had been coined by Malcolm McLaren in the late Eighties in reference to a Fifties-style bullet bra worn on the outside of a sweatshirt he had designed with Vivienne Westwood. Madonna was an early pioneer of the trend, most famously when she took to the stage on her 1990 Blond Ambition Tour in Jean Paul Gaultier's cone bra.

The new millennium heralded the return of the sexy model, personified by the statuesque Brazilian Gisele Bündchen. As a Victoria's Secret Angel, she modelled the brand's hyper-sexy

↑ "Slip dressing is back," Ellie Pithers announced on Vogue. co.uk after seeing the Spring/ Summer 2016 collections of Saint Laurent, Givenchy, Calvin Klein, Céline and Burberry celebrate a re-emergence of the formerly discreet undergarment that transitioned to a fully fledged dress in its own right in the Nineties. For the cover of the February 2016 issue, Dakota Johnson, star of the film *Fifty Shades of Grey* (2015), wears Phoebe Philo for Céline's leather and lace iteration and wool jacket, styled by Kate Phelan.

feminine lingerie and generated headlines in 2000 when she walked the runway in a ruby-and-diamond-encrusted bra and knickers – the most expensive underwear set ever. "For years underwear was a surreal and separate world," noted Susan Irvine in *Vogue* in May 2002, "now it's fashion's new playground."

Everyone, it seemed, was selling lingerie – from niche boutiques and labels such as Agent Provocateur, Myla, Coco de Mer, Bodas, Frost French and Topshop to designers including Prada, Alberta Ferretti, Chloé, Clements Ribeiro and John Galliano, and high-street stalwart Marks & Spencer (from where one in four British women buy their underwear today).

Where to now? For some, cosmetic surgery has become a tool to "fix" perceived and actual bodily flaws, and, in so doing, has taken over from some of the original purpose of underpinnings (but, perversely, has given new impetus to show off the resculpted body). Although the immense power of social media and its clever filters can reinforce sexual stereotypes and facilitate overly perfect representations of ourselves, increasingly it is being used to defy traditional ideals. Designers and advertisers have been called out for airbrushing photographs, and overt sexuality is being challenged by brands that encourage vulnerability and imperfections. We are dialling down our expectations of perfection and celebrating a more natural body shape.

"Real" bodies are being used in advertising campaigns, and women are embracing a more natural look supported by the popular rise in feminism and the pursuit of "healthier" body shapes. Attitudes toward gender and sexuality are changing – in 2015 Caitlyn Jenner marked her debut as a transgender woman wearing a satin corset on the cover of *Vanity Fair*. In 2017 Serena Rees, Agent Provocateur's co-founder, launched a new line of gender-neutral underwear, Les Girls Les Boys, a world away from AP's upfront glamour. It was, she explained in *Vogue*, "about a cross-cultural mindset and fluid sexual identities."

Lingerie is nothing if not adaptive. Deployed variously as a weapon of seduction, concealment, physical constraint, a challenge to convention and a celebration of femininity, in little more than a hundred years we have moved from the deforming, constricting S-bend-style corset to a "smart" bra that can track biometric data and send it to your mobile phone. Whatever comes next, it would be hard to argue against the reassurance of knowing one's undies are "absolutely and impeccably right".

→ There is an element of historical dress-up in this February 1991 image of Helena Christensen. Styled by Sarajane Hoare, it is an amalgam of principal boy and ship's figurehead. The mood is matched by the irreverent spirit of Vivienne Westwood's peek-a-bow floral-print corset, the Lycra pants from Debut Dancewear and thigh-high silk-satin boots by Jean Paul Gaultier.

stretch
& go

← A body in a body. Almost
abstract in its near-monochrome
simplicity, the composition of
this image from June 1988, with
its focus on the model's torso,
captures at once two defining
themes of the Eighties: the
sartorial touchstone that was
the bodysuit and the athletic
power of the body itself. A
multitasking version of a leotard,
the bodysuit was designed to show
off curves while creating a smooth
base when worn with trousers or
skirts. In this silk/elastane body by
Nikos, with its crossover front and
back, and wide built-in belt, the
contrast of the sharp linearity of
the "V" back and the long, gentle
high-cut curve across the hips
suggest a combination of strength
and flexibility.

It's hard to overestimate the importance of man-made fibres in the development of modern lingerie – and with our knicker drawers today filled with light-as-a-feather, barely-there confections, it's clear that we have come on leaps and bounds since The Rational Dress Society declared, in 1881, that "no woman should have to wear more than 7lb [3.2 kg] of underwear".

Diet and exercise tips often accompanied lingerie features in *Vogue*'s early years, the effect of which, intended or otherwise, was the inference of a connection between underwear and fitness and wellbeing. Who could resist the headline "How to Look Five Pounds Lighter" on a page of the latest lingerie designs? In January 1960, *Vogue* promised this could be achieved with, "A little vanity, a little will-power – and only an ounce or two of Lycra or Vyrene."

Three fibres in particular have allowed for significant advances in the comfort and durability of underwear. Rayon, the world's first man-made fibre, was produced from cellulose extracted from wood pulp and could be blended with other fibres to create a variety of finishes. First made commercially in 1905, it became known as "artificial silk" in the Twenties when its use in hosiery, lingerie and clothing appealed to women who could not afford the real thing.

Nylon, launched by US chemical company DuPont in 1939, was an instant hit, especially for stockings. Whereas rayon was prone to wrinkles and tears, nylon was strong, easy to wash, drip-dry and provided prettiness without being fragile. In the words of the company's vice-president at the time, Charles Stine, it was "strong as steel, as fine as a spider's web".

But the real game-changer was Lycra, another DuPont product. Invented in 1958, it provided strength, elasticity and an ability to return to its original shape after stretching. No wonder *Vogue* described it, in 1961, as a miracle. "Any girdle that's made of it will be one-third lighter than a similar girdle that isn't and not a whit less strong."

In March 1964, the word "elasometric" first appeared in *Vogue*, defined as "all those trade names given to the marvellous non-rubber man-made elastics that are stronger and lighter than anything in nature". In 1968, the magazine encouraged readers to "drive, jump, ride, stretch, accelerate into spring with briefer, simpler foundations that you can put on and forget. They look like you, move like you, feel like you."

Underwear remained firmly hidden beneath clothes until the Seventies, when it started to become more visible, thanks to the increased interest in exercise and the popularity of aerobics. Lycra became a vital part of the sporting wardrobe. The first exercise-specific bra, brought out in 1977, was initially called a "jockbra" and was specifically designed to prevent chafing. The first prototype was two jockstraps sewn together.

As working out boomed in the Eighties, Lycra really came into its own. Its flexible properties were instrumental in advances in the form and function of underwear as well as high fashion and athletic wear, through much publicized collaborations with designers such as Giorgio di Sant'Angelo and Norma Kamali, as well as with athletes such as Andre Agassi and Michael Jordan. Traditional underwear garments began to influence designs for outerwear, with leotards, bustiers and panty girdles morphing into bodysuits, tube tops and cycling shorts.

Muscles became acceptable, even desirable, and a much more sexually mature, curvaceous woman emerged, her legs elongated by the new high-cut knicker styles. As a reaction against lacy lingerie and the push-up Wonderbra, Calvin Klein began a trend for locker-room underwear for women with his launch in 1984 of boxer shorts complete with a three-button fly and wide waistband. *Time* magazine called them "Calvin's New Gender Benders".

Boundaries between clothing designed for sports and casual daywear soon began to blur. In the June 1988 issue of *Vogue*, Sarah Mower noted, "The intrigue of underwear has surfaced as a major preoccupation in the fashion of the Eighties. So closely has contemporary clothing been concerned with revealing the lines of the body that the structure of outerwear has surreptitiously annexed the form and fabric of underwear. New garments have evolved – the bodysuit, the bra that is half T-shirt, boxer shorts made for a woman and often worn on the beach – who can say which is what?"

The trend continued. In the December 1997 issue, *Vogue* highlighted a move toward "lifestyle undressing", noting activity-specific lingerie lines catering for "everything from skiing in Zermatt to dining in splendour, the definitive piece of lifestyle lingerie being La Perla's 'sculpture' bra, renowned for invisibly underpinning the classic white tee".

The overriding trend in fashion now is "athleisure" – a hybrid of sports-, street- and daywear. Traditional performance sportswear companies have adopted a more fashion-led approach to their collections, forging collaborations with designers and celebrities, such as Adidas with Stella McCartney, Raf Simons with Pharrell Williams, Nike with Virgil Abloh, and Puma with Kylie Jenner and Rihanna. Meanwhile, luxury brands are teaming up with streetwear labels and sporting bodies – to wit, Louis Vuitton and Supreme, Gucci and Major League Baseball.

Dress codes in the workplace are more relaxed and there is a desire to dress for comfort as well as style. The latest innovations in textiles technology are allowing garments to become more breathable and lightweight, merging with the functionality of gymwear. In underwear terms this translates as less structure and more comfort, as seen in the enormous popularity of bralettes and generously cut knickers over underwired push-up bras and thongs.

Undoubtedly, the health boom will continue, and technology will ensure ever more sophisticated fabrics, but before we get too cosy and comfortable in our cropped bra tops and tracksuit trousers, it would be wise to heed a remark about the perversity of fashion in the February 1991 issue of *Vogue*. Sarah Mower wrote that fashion "has an escapist exaggeration-ist, plain naughty instinct. In times when the pressure is on to produce slouchy, wearable, comfortable, sporty clothes that might be worn by either sex, there's a little demon jigging about in the corner of the fashion imagination that says, to hell with that – let's do something uncomfortable, wicked, erotic, extreme!"

↑ In the earlier issues of *Vogue*, lingerie fashion stories were often combined with exercise tips because "the look of a dress depends, as always, on the figure beneath – lifted bust, flat stomach, compact waist. Lovely lingerie does something to a woman's morale; simple exercises, regularly performed, do even more." Given that two of the three models in this illustration for "Lingerie and Limbering" in the August 1948 issue wear long petticoats, it is just as well that the prescribed exercises aren't too vigorous. The illustrator, Anthony Gilbert, worked at the advertising agency J. Walter Thompson, where he created some of the most iconic images of 20th-century marketing, including the ornate clock on the After Eight chocolate mints box.

→ This page in the April 1961 issue was dedicated to "light, decidedly comfortable foundations ready to enter into partnership with sports clothes", and the charming illustration by Bobby Hillson shows how stretching and body movement go hand in hand with stretchy fabrics. The star fabric here was Vyrene, "a new, non-perishable elastic yarn that gets dry overnight". Hillson was an important figure in post-war fashion illustration who worked for *Vogue* in the Sixties before going on to found the MA Fashion course at London's Central Saint Martins, where she tutored, among others, Alexander McQueen, Rifat Ozbek and John Galliano.

← By the middle of the fitness-obsessed Eighties, the craze for high-impact aerobics had caused enough injuries to orient the fitness trend toward a less intense, or low-impact, phase. In August 1986, in a feature entitled "Low Impact, High Energy: How Fit Do You Need to Be?", *Vogue*'s Deborah Hutton found that, "After the boom, second-stage fitness takes a measured approach." The model Claire Ringrose is shown in a more relaxed form of sportswear in "the optimum modern shape". She wears high-cut cotton pants by Joseph Pour La Danse while wielding chrome dumbbells.

↑ In the "*Vogue*'s Eye View of a Very Fast Mover" feature from 15 April 1969, we see an early hint of lingerie melding with sports clothing: "Sports clothes showed fashion how to be fast and free. Now they show how to steal the thunder from all the other competitors, with racing colours, great goggle glasses, hair binders, all-in-ones, second-skin shapes, striding shorts." In a spear-wielding pose suggestive of a stylized tribal dance, the model wears a pink ciré punctuation bra, described as "two dots and a dash", and combined shorts and skirt, known today as a skort.

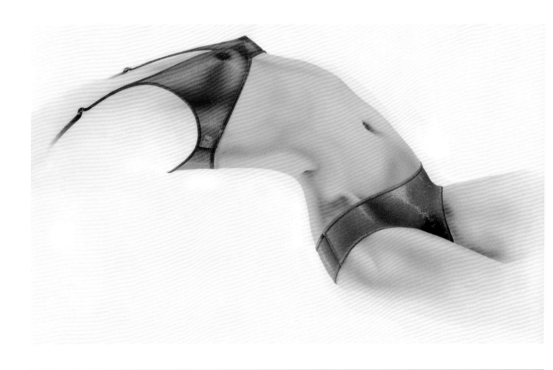

↑ The Pop-Art style of the April 1972 feature "A Bright Girl's Guide to Starting Summer", by graphic artist Michael English, brilliantly conveys the glossy sheerness of the seamless bra and knickers, while the model's arched back and the shadow of just visible nipples and pubic hair give the image a strong sexual charge. "If you want to run, jump, and feel free this summer, begin here," suggests the caption. "New bras and pants look like expensive bikinis: brief, functional, brilliantly coloured. Mies van der Rohe as opposed to Louis XIV. Bras get their shape from the cut and stretch but mainly from you, and they're V-shaped. The fabrics are thin as handkerchiefs."

→ Play clothes or underclothes? As seen here in January 1970, the tilt of the model's hips and length of her legs are accentuated by the optical stripes of the red, white and blue handkerchief bra, boxer shorts and knee socks in Helanca nylon stretchy lace, designed by Sixties fashion phenomenon Mary Quant.

Her aesthetic was influenced by dancers, musicians and the street chic of the Chelsea set, and she created high-fashion versions of the outfits she had worn as a child at school and at dance classes. She pioneered the miniskirt and paired her very short dresses perfectly with her hosiery and underwear range.

← This scarlet nylon tricot bra, softly seamed, with pin-thin elastic straps, worn with a scarlet and striped Lycra panty girdle, both by Warner's, featured in the 15 September 1967 issue. The yarn in tricot is knitted vertically, rather than in single rows, which makes it very resistant to runs and well suited to use in lingerie. This picture ran in *Vogue*'s "Young Ideas" pages, which had been started in 1962 by *Vogue*

Editor Beatrix Miller as a way of incorporating less sophisticated clothes and younger models, captured in a more modern style, into the magazine.

↑ Mary Quant launched her first lingerie collection, one of the very first to incorporate Lycra, in 1965. It was all in black and white, so that every bra and girdle would work together, as seen here in the 1 March issue of that year.

The new man-made elastics, such as Lycra, were not only exceptionally strong and light but, as *Vogue* comments, "They take the dye too, another reason for the easy-match development." Such advances in fabrication resulted in "a lighter, freer shape to foundations".

↑ "Soak up some winter sun in high-performance sportswear with a tropical twist." The jersey bra top and shorts by Red Valentino, as seen in January 2018, could just as easily be worn under a tracksuit as for a game of beach volleyball or catching some rays on a cool watermelon pool inflatable. The image shows just how blurred the lines have become between "off-duty" clothing, sportswear and lingerie.

→ With tousled curls, a long, lean figure and bags of attitude, Argentinian model Mica Argañaraz nails the 21st-century "athleisure" trend in a perfect high-low collision of activewear and comfort clothes, designer and streetwear. For this July 2016 image, styled by Kate Phelan, Chanel's cotton bra top and Calvin Klein underwear is teamed with an Adidas Originals track jacket, Maison Margiela silk jogging trousers with slashed hems, and Nike high tops.

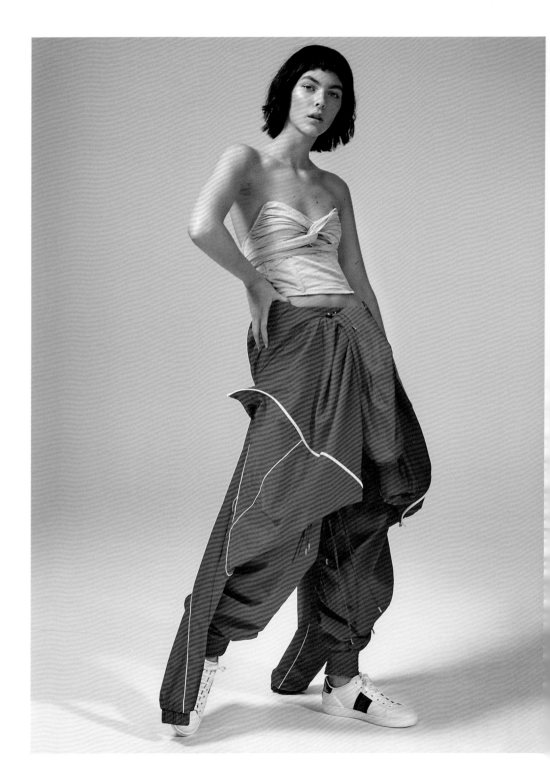

← The bustier gets a whole new lease of life when it's reinvented in grey jersey and breaks out from its traditional position beneath a dress or blouse. Here, in the April 2018 issue, worn with an athletic jacket and track pants, the result is a colour-blocked combination of sporty pragmatism and a feminine silhouette.

↑ In "Boot Camp", a military-inspired shoot with Brazilian model Raquel Zimmermann for the March 2010 issue, Kate Phelan blends desert uniform with men's locker-room style. The utility chic of the ruffle-collared jacket by Dior contrasts with the sporty undergarments in stretchy jersey fabrics worn beneath – cotton boxer briefs by Sloggi, Alexander Wang jersey top and American Apparel jersey leggings.

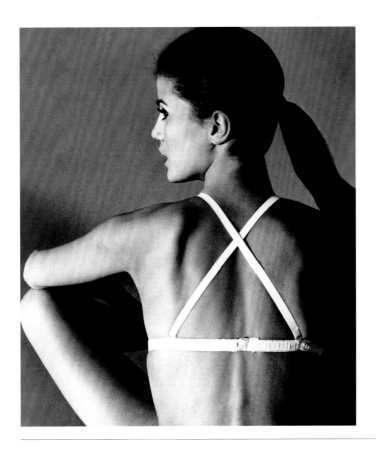

←← How better to illustrate the comfort and flexibility of the stretch lace Vyrene bra and girdle by Mistée than by photographing the model in the Reclining Hero yoga pose? In the 15 October 1965 issue, *Vogue* likens the lingerie to a firm second skin, which makes "the body look controlled but lithe, without the 'firm-girdled' look". It also notes key attributes of the story's "Heavenly Bodies" title as being "litheness of leg, a slim young-swimmer look to the shoulders, a flat young look to the waist and midriff. There is no need to have an obsession about a cinched-in waist. Bosoms are natural, round, with no hoist."

↑ The angular geometry of the model's body position mimics the linear straps that criss-cross her back. The bra by Warner's was included in a "Young Ideas" story called "Undercover Action" in the 15 April 1967 issue, which presented "light, lithe looks to leap about in". Later in the same story, there was a front-view picture of the bra, showing how to draw the straps together beneath the neck at the front, with the use of an optional strap, to allow the wearing of a shoulder-revealing dress.

→ A feature from 15 April 1965, called "The Revolution That's Rocked Foundations", debuted "the new body stocking" by Austrian designer Rudi Gernreich – a sheer and natural look with a deep, diving front, half cups of transparent nylon tricot, a skin-coloured net body and detachable suspenders. It was, according to the caption, "like a second skin… no bones, no wires about them. Instead everything body-shaped, skin-coloured, barely visible and beautifully free."

← The minimal simplicity of a plain grey stretch cotton leotard by Ralph Lauren is here shot as part of the summer story "Figures in Seascape" in Hawaii for May 1985. The high-cut leg was an Eighties signature style in underwear and swimwear, giving the twin benefits of slimming the waist and elongating the leg. Kim Kardashian and Bella Hadid were among a number of celebrities who spearheaded a revival of the style in swimwear in 2017.

↑ Actress, model and *Vogue*'s October 2017 cover star Zoë Kravitz skewers the reader with a look that reflects her formidable personality. In the accompanying story, "I Want to Be Bold", writer Hermione Eyre notes that Kravitz carved out her Hollywood career through hard work, persistence and an admirable unwillingness to compromise – an attitude matched by her posing in nothing but big, black satin pants by Eres.

↑ Fashion's new athleticism pervaded the Spring/Summer 2014 collections, and in the magazine's story "On Your Marks" from March 2014, *Vogue* proposes: "Here's the game plan: motivate your spring wardrobe now with pacy, high-definition separates and shots of authentic sportswear." The graffiti-covered wall in the background lends an urban grittiness to this photograph of model Sam Rollinson, wearing a black triangle bra beneath a black mesh vest and black silk-georgette trousers, all by Gucci designer Frida Giannini, and track top by Adidas Originals.

→ "Strip back to the athleticism of body-centric dressing and fast track yourself into a laddered miniskirt", reads the caption for this April 2010 photograph. Lara Stone wears an off-the-shoulder top layered over a bra with a curve-hugging pencil skirt, all by Mark Fast, and Nike high tops. The lattice criss-crossing on the stretch skirt references fishnet tights and corset lacing.

← In this May 1989 beauty story entitled "Brave, Wild Warrior Women Dress to Scare Off the Baddies", traditional lingerie textures are toughened up and the boundaries of under- and outerwear are blurred. Styled by Sarah Walter, the model wears a black leather halterneck bra top with a silver stud popper by Pam Hogg and black cotton and Lycra knickers by Jean Paul Gaultier.

↑ Cosmetic surgery offers the ultimate recourse to shaping one's body, and the glamorous January 1999 story "High Maintenance" shows that "attaining the body beautiful is no longer a fantasy". In a slightly disturbing image we see a woman in diamond jewellery, "marked up" for her procedure. Our view from behind the chair in the foreground suggests that it is shared with that of the doctor who will perform the surgery. The fact that her expensive black

La Perla underwear reveals an arguably perfect body heightens our discomfort and points to the complicated emotional and psychological reasons, not to mention financial wherewithal, that inform a woman's choice to go under the knife.

pretty things

For all the progress women have made toward emancipation and equality over the past century, it's hard to deny that there has been little change to the timeless appeal of beautiful, feminine lingerie. Women have long delighted in the romantic, sensuous loveliness of pretty underwear far beyond its quotidian function, both for its appearance and its indubitable mood-boosting properties.

When actress Anne-Marie Duff chose lingerie as her luxury on BBC Radio 4's *Desert Island Discs* in March 2018, she highlighted the psychological importance underwear has for many women. Faced with being cast away on the hypothetical island with no means of escape, she opted for some beautiful underwear ."I could run around in the most divine bra and pants and feel like a million dollars!" she said gleefully.

The images in this chapter celebrate the lacy lightness, transparency, sherbet colours and sheer girlie-ness that are complicit in defining lingerie at its most feminine. "Not only does it enhance one's clothes and figure, the word women most use to describe the boost that a silky something gliding over their skin gives them is 'confidence'," reported Plum Sykes in the June 1996 issue of *Vogue*.

Some may say that the tougher the fashion trend on the outside, the greater the need to counterbalance it with softer, gentler lingerie on the inside. Others feel that the wearing of beautiful things close to the skin provides the confidence to go out and conquer the world. Another view, expressed by *Vogue* in 1994, is that it is "a way for women to project their dream-visions

← Lucinda Chambers's styling evokes a Fifties bohemian air in this image from the May 2008 story "The Sheltering Sky", featuring generously cut Damaris briefs and bra in a charming, rose-strewn print, worn here by Jessica Stam. "Before Damaris, a bra was a bra, and a knicker was simply a knicker," said *Vogue* of Damaris Evans, the graduate from London's Central Saint Martins, who began her business in 2001 from her kitchen table and is best known for her much-copied bow-back knickers. "Avant-garde lingerie should be full of surprises," she says. "It must push design boundaries. Through lingerie a woman shows her true style. It is integral that my designs are luxurious, fun, interesting, cool and essentially functional."

of their own bodies". Whatever is in your knicker drawer – frilly, beribboned bralettes, slinky lace numbers gifted by husbands or lovers, a tangle of flesh-toned comfortable everyday pants and bras, or rose-strewn vintage-inspired confections – lingerie gives a form to our femininity.

There is an interesting correlation between lingerie's largely secret status and the influence it has had on outerwear, both in terms of details (lace, frills, boudoir colours, ribbons and bows) and, in some cases, the reinvention of traditional undergarments as outerwear in their own right. *Vogue* noted both these points in an October 1991 article about the autumn couture collections, featuring Yves Saint Laurent's panels of lace, Versace's lace petticoat dresses and Valentino's wizardry with barely-there silk charmeuse – all divine creations with exquisite appliqué, lace, transparency and featherweight fabrics. "The way bedroom secrets have moved on to the street must be the fashion phenomenon of our times," writer Rosie Martin observed.

The babydoll was originally invented as a short nightdress by Sylvia Pedlar, the American designer known as "the Dior of lingerie", in response to fabric shortages during World War II. Its trapeze shape became one of Cristóbal Balenciaga's couture codes. During the Sixties, the shape informed playful A-line silhouettes that contributed to many fashion-forward young women looking rather childlike, dressed in short lengths, pinafores and gymslips. The dress became a leitmotif of the "kinderwhore" look of female grunge bands in the Nineties. By wearing babydoll dresses and flower crowns with chunky boots during her chaotic and reckless stage performances with her band Hole, Courtney Love co-opted the style to parody the "good-girl" aesthetic and infantilization of women.

Bra tops are commonplace and nobody blinks an eye at a corset worn as a top with jeans or a skirt (see next chapter). Big pants have extended their constituency far beyond granny's drawers. We may still be happy to defer to Batman as the true champion of wearing them on the outside – that is, over the top of tights – but they have come to the fore in the 2010s. As Vogue.co.uk acknowledged in April 2016, "a pair of proper pants visible beneath body-skimming layers is now an established style code for evening wear".

The garment to have made the most successful transfer from under- to outerwear is the slip dress. Elizabeth Taylor drew attention to it in sultry scenes in *Cat on a Hot Tin Roof* (1958) and

Butterfield 8 (1960), when she wore nothing but an ivory slip and high heels. Although a simple slip was an everyday undergarment for women of the time, Taylor imbued it with an off-the-charts sexy factor. (In *Butterfield 8*, it was considered to be so provocative to movie-goers that the costume designer had to construct a special lining for it to ensure the actress's modesty.)

Cut short in the Sixties, the slip largely faded out in the Seventies when designers made clothing with built-in linings. It emerged as a fully fledged dress in its own right in 1993, when Kate Moss was photographed at a model agency party wearing a transparent silver slip by Liza Bruce. With a beer bottle and a Marlboro Light as accessories, and her friend Naomi Campbell at her side, it was a picture of insouciant style.

Meanwhile, John Galliano was refining and reviving the bias-cutting technique Madame Vionnet had used in the Thirties for her evening gowns to create his signature designs. Appearing on the catwalk at Christian Dior and as a navy-blue gown worn by Diana, Princess of Wales, at the 1996 Met Gala, the slip was instantly propelled to the status of fashion phenomenon.

The slip is now a wardrobe staple, an intensely feminine piece because of how it delicately skims the body. Its essential simplicity means that it can be styled in any number of ways – worn very simply and unadorned, as seen in the photographs in this chapter, or layered and styled to the max. "Wear yours with a sturdy ankle boot, or second-skin thigh-high if you're feeling brave," suggested Vogue.co.uk in November 2015. "A mannish blazer or chunky cardigan will play the whole ensemble down while you're waiting for the Uber to arrive."

So lingerie is no longer confined to existing exclusively in a hidden realm. It's totally OK to slide a Stella McCartney lace-trimmed camisole underneath one of her crisply tailored jackets, or arrive at an event wearing a Prada bra top. But whatever underwear's new sartorial trajectories, it's unlikely that its special place in (and next to) a woman's heart will change. The late Marie Colvin testified to the uplifting benefits beautiful underwear can provide when she explained in the December 2004 issue of *Vogue* the extreme incongruity of her love of exquisite La Perla lingerie and her work as a war correspondent: "If I have lace, beautiful lingerie under all the muck and tiredness, I, and I alone, know it's there and somehow it cheers me."

← Long associated with femininity, sweetness and romance, from the palest flesh tones so popular in the Twenties and Thirties, through rose, to watermelon, flamingo, fuchsia and neon, pink has been a staple colour choice for lingerie. In this photograph from November 2015, French actress and Bond girl Léa Seydoux is ostensibly primly attired in Christopher Kane's straight skirt and cable-knit Aran cardigan, worn with a brooch.

But by unbuttoning her cardigan, Kate Phelan (who styled this image) disrupts her perfect poise by drawing our focus to the satin and tulle Fifi Chachnil bra with the tiny bow and the beguiling lingerie details of the lace overlay on her satin pencil skirt, pivoting the image from pretty to seductive.

↑ "Pink, from palest to rose to brilliant persimmon and intense fuchsia, has grown up to become winter's spotlight colour," says *Vogue* in the "Make Me Blush" feature for November 2007. The silk triangle Passion Bait bra and Oasis knitted French knickers are "pure pin-up", tamed by the pearly-buttoned cardigan.

↑ These illustrations by Antonio Lopez, from the "Halter the Way You Look" feature in the 1 September 1972 issue, show a young Paloma Picasso wearing different examples of the new style of halterneck bra, by Janet Reger, Maidenform, Lovable and Kayser. Paloma, the caption reads, is a "designer of furs and jewels, and lives and works wonders in Paris. Halter bras will do the same for you." The artist, generally known only by his first name, was a charismatic, glamorous figure at the centre of the disco era, and an early advocate in the fashion industry of embracing inclusivity and diversity. He made the models in his drawings confident and sexy, and, in so doing, bucked the trend for photography as the dominant medium in fashion media, giving fashion illustration a reboot.

→ This June 1996 image of a simple, sheer, cocoa underwired bra and briefs by Charnos accompanied a feature called "Undertherapy", extolling the feel-good factor that beautiful underwear can engender. Plum Sykes posits that "an hour-long session at London underwear specialist Rigby & Peller apparently has more uplifting powers than all the hypno-, hydro- and seaweed therapies put together…"

↑ "Too much practical lingerie makes a dull woman. An occasional frill is good for the soul," advised *Vogue* in 1932. This counsel still holds in this February 2018 image of Diane Kruger in a silk-satin playsuit (or camiknickers, as the garment, a combination of a camisole and French knickers, was first called in the Twenties) by Rosamosario. One of a portfolio of images styled by British *Vogue*'s Editor-in-Chief, Edward Enninful, and photographed at the time of Hollywood's re-evaluation of itself in the wake of the Harvey Weinstein scandal, it celebrates a group of strong female actors whose recent film roles stand out as representative of the new mood in Tinseltown.

→ "Everything's happening at once, everyone's coming to dinner," reads the caption in the "Bright Girl's Guide to the Red Hot Style" feature from August 1979. The harried hostess, clearly not enamoured of having to iron her dress before getting the party started, nonetheless delivers the aforementioned style in a cherry-red silk and white lace slip by Charlotte Hilton. The slip was still considered an undergarment in the late Seventies, but can be worn as a dress today and no one would bat an eyelid.

←← Style is often the catalyst for social revolution. Here, in "As Time Goes By" from *Vogue*'s centenary issue (June 2016), Lucinda Chambers captures the newfound freedom of the Bright Young Things of the Roaring Twenties. Sam Rollinson shines in Pam Hogg's jewelled hot pants, Bebaroque jewelled stockings and bra by What Katie Did, beneath Erdem's feather cape. Out with complicated updos, tightly laced corsets, binding girdles and ample petticoats, and in with bob cuts and simple, unstructured bra tops and high-waisted knickers.

↑ Midway through the Seventies, the minimal triangle bra, bikini pants and functional styles of the previous decade began to give way to more romantic designs in French silks and lace, popularized by Janet Reger, as shown fourth from the left. The Gossard bra, far right, with Wonderlift padding, suggests the shape of things to come. The model in this "Under All the Bare Minimum" feature from 15 March 1975 is Cheryl Tiegs, often described as the first American supermodel.

→ "Bras have been like something you wear on your head New Year's Eve," commented Rudi Gernreich. In contrast, his 1965 "no-bra bra", as featured in January 1965, was the essence of simplicity, perfect for the spare look of sexually liberated mid-Sixties fashion. It had neither wire nor padding, and was made of bias-cut nylon tricot, simply darted, thereby adapting to the natural form of the breasts.

↑ Dennis Davidson's illustration for "The Underlying Facts" feature in June 1986 shows a simple, unstructured satin bra and Bermuda knickers to match, both by Norma Kamali. Long before the term "athleisure" was so much as a twinkle in a marketing director's eye, the legendary New York-born designer was building her business on stretchy, eminently wearable styles for the Studio 54 set and beyond.

→ Chronicling her quest to find the perfect bra to fit her figure in the August 2004 issue, Daisy Garnett struck gold with a made-to-measure confection by Parisian corsetière Cadolle. She had imagined "a bells and whistles bra; all lace and uplift, bows and cleavage. Instead, I came away with something rather plain, made from the palest pink nylon netting (netting is stronger and more durable than lace or silk,

and has the added advantage of lying absolutely flush against the skin)."

← "Underclothes, if any, are pretty, coloured, transparent," declared *Vogue* in June 1971. For the free spirit of the Seventies, underwear was optional, but if she felt like wearing, say, a transparent lime-green bra and pants appliquéd with puce sailing boats from Emmanuelle Khanh, azure-coloured stockings and a glass bead necklace, why ever not? Challenging the rules was the theme of this shoot entitled "*Vogue*'s New Beauty Etiquette".

It left the reader in no doubt as to how to respond to old-school diktats, such as, "A lady never wears fake jewels, coloured underwear, diamonds before breakfast." The model Cathee Dahmen had been discovered in her late teens by the *New York Times* illustrator Antonio Lopez (see page 46). She epitomized the cultural movement of the Sixties dubbed "Youthquake" by American *Vogue*'s Diana Vreeland.

↑ Cool blue lingerie takes the plunge in this July 1992 high-summer story "Beach Babe", styled by Jayne Pickering and shot at The Breakers hotel at Palm Beach in Florida. Karen Mulder wears a scalloped turquoise lace underwired bra and matching lace briefs by La Perla.

← There is a bohemian feeling to this image in the fashion feature "Rainbow Warriors" from May 1996. Adorned in colourful beaded jewellery, Amber Valletta wears Gianni Versace's unmistakable and imaginative take on the slip dress for his Summer 1996 couture collection. Black lace is used to embellish a metal mesh "fabric" called Oroton, which he had developed in the early Eighties to give the impression of the body being encased in liquid metal, recalling classical draperies.

↑ The June 1993 story "Under-exposure", styled by Cathy Kasterine, sparked a huge outcry over child sexualization and exploitation. The pictures were a world away from the prevailing style of lingerie fashion, which was altogether glossier and sexier. Kate Moss, with her slight physique, make-up-free face and no discernible bust, projected a vulnerability at odds with the upbeat confidence of the ruling class of supermodels (Linda, Christy and Naomi). The caption

answered the question "What to wear beneath effort-free clothes?" with "Barely-there underwear, naturally." British *Vogue*'s Editor-in-Chief at the time Alexandra Shulman said it was a balancing act: "I didn't want people to look tragic, druggy, sick or too thin. I was searching for a fashion look that was more naturalistic."

← ← In the December 2007 "Glamour" issue of *Vogue*, Naomi Campbell and Claudia Schiffer indulge in the ultimate girlie catch-up in a suite at The Dorchester, London. Both wear silk kimonos as coverups. Claudia's silk bra is by Jean Yu, an American lingerie designer whose signature bra style is a simple triangle in a feather-light fabric, such as chiffon, charmeuse or georgette, in a pale colour, to reference the Twenties but with a modern aesthetic. Naomi is clad in Agent Provocateur, and, as the caption reads, "Nobody does it better. From Mayfair to Holborn, Naomi Campbell takes on London in her inimitable, fabulous style."

↑ In this November 1975 image, the spotlight is thrown on pastel-peach silk crepe de chine and burnt-apricot lace brasserie and French knickers, by Keturah Brown, the latter cut to lie flat on the hips. The (then) new label was by Goug Wilcox, who, after designing evening wear in Rome and for Bellville Sassoon, spotted a gap in the market for lingerie made of natural fibres. The style of French knickers evolved from the baggy, long-legged drawers of the Victorian era. Very popular in the Twenties and Thirties, they fell out of fashion in the Forties and Fifties in favour of briefs, partly due to fabric shortages, only to be revived in the Seventies by Janet Reger before losing favour again in the Nineties, when briefs and thongs became more popular.

→ Anouck Lepère wears a dusty-blue silk-chiffon bra and matching French knickers by Prada. This May 2002 image was part of a feature called "Knickerbocker Glory", in which Susan Irvine examined the lingerie boom. "The kind of emotion women used to reserve for shoes is being poured out on the new universe of self-expression that is underwear," she noted.

← The peach satin, heart-shaped pillow, with its lace trim, gives a slightly saccharine edge to this photograph from the 1 April 1978 issue. The silk crepe de chine camisole and knickers, with a smattering of hand-painted flowers, are by Helen Radok.

↑ In an oversized hat befitting Edward Lear's Quangle Wangle, model Liberty Ross sits on a rumpled bed in a pleated chiffon camisole over an ice-blue silk-satin and lace underwired bra, both by Myla. "Bedroom games are best played in the sweetest of silk nothings, and the new, barely-there lingerie," teases *Vogue* in the January 2004 issue.

→ → The year's "triumphant trio" – Suki Waterhouse, Cara Delevingne and Georgia May Jagger – appear in the "Candy Coated" feature in April 2015. "Right now, we're crushing big on pretty," *Vogue*

admits in the accompanying text. "We've developed a new-found enthusiasm for deliciously playful candy colours that sweeten up the scene via tiered tulle party frocks and babydoll dresses; fun flights of fancy that prove irresistible among girlfriends." Except for Georgia May's La Perla lace bra and Cara's Agent Provocateur bra and knickers, all the clothing is by Parisienne lingerie designer Fifi Chachnil, whose creations draw on vintage silhouettes and cabaret traditions.

↑ This all-in-one silk-satin bloomer
suit, or teddy, edged with lace,
by Julia at Charles Grahame,
featured in the November 1982
issue. The garment was a revival
of the classic styles that had gone
out of fashion during the "mod"
Sixties, and provided a feminine,
sexy counterpoint to men's power
suits and the big shoulder pads that
many women were wearing. Worn
with a cashmere cardigan and
pearls – what else?

→ Packing for a holiday or vacation
has to be easy. In the July 1998
feature "Taking the Heat out of
Hot Weather Dressing", *Vogue*
suggests taking only "a handful
of pared-down timeless pieces",
including "a slip of satin dress
with perfect bias". Shot at the
Royal Pavilion hotel in St James,
Barbados, this photograph shows
Susan Miner in an ivory ankle-
length slip and loose white linen
duster coat, both by Ellis Flyte.

← In the August 1994 story "Small Wonder", styled by Tiina Laakkonen, cover star Kate Moss wears a long, silver-mix, bias-cut slip dress by Edina Ronay. It marked the beginning of the model's obsession with slip dresses, to which *Vogue* devoted a story in March 2018. Of the slip dress she wore in Stella McCartney's graduate show in 1995, she said, "I loved it when she did dresses that looked like lingerie."

↑ "Spring beckons, and our favourite shop floors will soon be bursting with new looks. What to expect?" In February 2016, *Vogue* heralded barely-there, lingerie-inspired, slippery silk slip dresses as key to spring style. In a feature entitled "First Light", model Damaris Goddrie plunges into the water in a Burberry Prorsum slip dress with cording, styled by Francesca Burns.

↑ In this feature from May 1991,
showing cool colours for a summer
evening, *Vogue* suggests this
bias-cut satin-backed crepe slip
by Jenny Packham. "Tenderly
traced across naked shoulders,
the shoelace strap gives the shift
dress all the delicate sex appeal
of lingerie."

→ A cardinal rule when shooting
the fashion pages of *Vogue* is not
to photograph the same thing more
than once, especially not for the
same issue. In some cases, when
a particular designer's collection is
universally heralded as important
or season-defining, it can be a
difficult situation to avoid, because
fashion editors may feel that a
particular look encapsulates their
story. Evidence of the rule being
broken came in "Rocket Girl", in

which the Edina Ronay slip dress
worn by Kate Moss (see page 70)
appeared again in the same August
1994 issue, this time styled by Kate
Phelan on Amber Valletta.

under control

"Probably the most controversial garment in the entire history of fashion," said fashion historian Valerie Steele of the corset in *The Corset: A Cultural History* (2003). It's true – mention of it provokes delight and dismay – but is it a tool of control and subjugation, or the apogee of the feminine form? Our enduring fascination with corsets has been perpetuated by literary and film heroines, from Madame Bovary to Scarlett O'Hara, and by the ever-popular heaving-bosom television costume dramas. More recently, corsets have become stage-show favourites of first-name-only pop divas, such as Madonna, Beyoncé, Kylie and Rihanna.

Fans argue that they encourage good posture and elongate the spine, that they show the bust to best advantage (indeed, they particularly suit fuller-figured women with a bust to fill them), and that their unboned and shorter modern iterations worn with jeans can be a jaunty alternative to a T-shirt or blouse.

Detractors liken them to sartorial prison cells, tight and stifling, promoted by Victorian values and forced upon women by men. But not so fast, says Steele – men, in fact, protested that the corset induced hysteria and health problems but women freely chose to wear them as an indicator of status and a way to attract the opposite sex. Then again, the corset's purpose was to minimize the waist by accentuating the curve between it and the bust and hips, thereby moulding the body into the "ideal" hourglass figure.

As *Vogue* beauty director Kathy Phillips explained in April 2001, studies into physical attractiveness have shown that men are more drawn to a woman with a "hand-span" waist measurement

← The 2001 film *Moulin Rouge!*, starring Nicole Kidman as Satine, the *belle époque* cabaret actress and courtesan, was the inspiration behind *Vogue*'s "The New Vic" story in the October 2001 issue, which explored fashion's new obsession with hourglass silhouettes and Victoriana. The Agent Provocateur corset is worn here in a decidedly 21st-century way – with woollen leggings.

– "women whose waists are 70 percent the size of their hips are rated by scientists as the most attractive to men of every culture". (Twiggy, Marilyn Monroe, Sophia Loren, the Venus de Milo, Elle Macpherson and Kate Moss all reportedly have this waist-to-hip ratio.) As well as being attractive to the opposite sex, this ratio is thought to be optimum for higher fertility and lower rates of chronic disease. Perhaps this is why the hourglass figure has enduring potency: the bottle for Schiaparelli's 1936 Shocking perfume was based on a cast of Mae West's body; Jean Paul Gaultier's Classique scent came in a pink glass bottle in the shape of a corseted woman; and Kim Kardashian West's KKW Body fragrance flacon was based on a mould of her own curvaceous body.

Fetishwear became a trend in the Eighties and Nineties when corsets were adopted by punks and worn as outerwear as a symbol of rebellion and sexual perversity. Vivienne Westwood put them on the fashion runway and they began to be reclaimed as trophies of female glamour and power. While her references were the bodices of the 18th century, the stays and bustles of the *belle époque* inspired Christian Lacroix. His amazing couture debut, a flamboyant collection of bubble skirts, extravagant fabrics and clashing colours, was made only months before the 1987 economic crash. For feminists such as Susan Faludi, it represented a low point in the reactionary Reagan/Thatcher decade, during which the advances toward social, political and economic emancipation for women made in the Seventies had been reversed. Her view was that Lacroix's fashion was frilly, fantasy clothes to be worn by women wanting to dress up as little girls. Others, however, considered it a knowingly ironic reappropriation of petticoats, corsets and stockings from a pre-feminist era.

Madonna's 1990 Blond Ambition world tour moved the dial further. Her performances of "Express Yourself" and "Like a Virgin" while wearing Jean Paul Gaultier's memorable rocket cone corsets and simulating masturbation challenged social mores on many levels and have become seminal images of pop culture.

Despite being declared outmoded and obsolete at the beginning of the 20th century, the corset has since had two big revivals. The first began in the late Thirties (although interrupted by the war), peaked in 1947 with the New Look, and continued throughout the Fifties, when the promotion of an exaggeratedly feminine figure was in keeping with the prevalent view that women should give up the paid employment they had undertaken as part of the war effort and return to the home. The second came in the Eighties and Nineties. Its disappearance in between was prompted by the continually changing "ideal" female silhouette, and whether the fashion was to enhance or conceal the waist. Nonetheless, it has continued to influence fashion and the category of lingerie that grew out of it, known as contour- or shapewear.

In the February 1993 issue, Rosie Martin extolled the latest generation of thigh-slimming, stomach-flattening, bust-boosting, contouring control underwear, explaining that, despite similarities to corsetry of the Fifties – deep gym knickers, broad-strapped bustier bras with wedge inserts to pump up the bosom, and bodyslips with and without suspenders – it was the new fibres, particularly Lycra, that were making the difference. Fabrics, even lace, could now stretch lengthwise as well as breadthwise, supporting, rather than constricting, the muscles. The new fabrics were lighter and therefore cooler than before.

This sort of flexibility solved numerous problems, celebrated by Alice B-B in *Vogue*'s November 2006 issue when she listed a host of ways in which it could help override errant lumps and bumps. Backless silk jersey dress? No problem – get a Donna Karan backless thong body. Protruding nipples? Try a moulded T-shirt bra. Chunky thighs? Slim Cognito Seamless Mid-thigh Shaper by Spanx is the answer. Desirous of a more generous bosom? A balconette bra is the thing. Modern-day stretchy, soft, padded, supporting underwear really does have all the bases covered.

In the 21st century, a new generation is exploring corsetry. The inspirations are myriad: an increased interest in burlesque, Kim Kardashian's waist-optimizing enthusiams, the success of E L James's 2011 bestseller *Fifty Shades of Grey*, Lily James's impossibly tiny waist in Disney's *Cinderella* (2015), and bravura corset-clad stage performances by Lady Gaga and Beyoncé. And when Miuccia Prada included cotton corset belts in her Autumn 2016 collection – worn on the outside of tailored garments made of menswear fabrics – it was probably not with seduction in mind but more likely as a sign that the corset has been reclaimed by women who are dressing for themselves.

↑ Linda Evangelista vamps it up in a black velvet and satin corset from Bellville Sassoon Lorcan Mullany and jet jewellery. Her short, tousled hair and open-armed toting of a feather boa lend a modern attitude to the period fashion; the caption from November 1993 reads, "the surprise is when serious Victorian elements are coupled with coquettish behaviour".

→ This floral and spotted lace-panelled, boned bodice and matching lace briefs, both by La Perla, featured in the January 1991 issue: "Black is the starting point for provocative pieces of sensual texture, that define bodylines and give an erogenous edge to curvaceous lingerie." Founded by corset-maker Ada Masotti in 1954, La Perla – the name of which was inspired by the red velvet-lined box in which the lingerie was

presented, like precious jewels – is one of the few historical Italian fashion houses to have been launched by a woman. Her use of exquisite fabrics and hand-stitched detail to marry sophistication and sexiness, and an ability to innovate to keep pace with changes in fashion – she introduced strong colours in the Sixties and stretch lace in the Seventies – helped to make the company one of the go-to brands for super-luxurious lingerie.

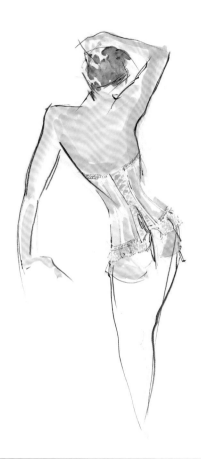

← A modern-day classical muse.
In this February 1988 photograph,
Christy Turlington wears Vivienne
Westwood's scooped, boned,
swathed cream silk jersey bodice,
a seductive meeting of corset and
goddess drapery, curved down to
a zip at the back.

↑ For the June 1986 issue,
Dennis Davidson illustrated "the
quintessential corset in white
satin – boned, laced, structured
to shape and made to measure, at
Rigby & Peller". The gold standard
in lingerie boutiques, Rigby &
Peller opened in London's South

Molton Street in 1939. It built its
reputation on its "proper" fitting
service, rigorous discretion and
patronage by everyone from
Margaret Thatcher and Gwyneth
Paltrow to Lady Gaga and Queen
Elizabeth II (to whom it was official
lingerie supplier until 2018, when
the Royal Warrant was withdrawn
after Buckingham Palace allegedly
deemed the publication of owner
June Kenton's 2017 *Storm in
a D-Cup* autobiography too
revelatory).

→ → This image, from the Spring/
Summer 1953 Beauty supplement,
focuses on good grooming and
reflects the emphasis on women's
femininity in the post-war years.
"Good grooming is to the body
what a good make-up is to the
face. It gives a sense of wellbeing
and self-confidence…Having dealt
with grooming, think about body
moulding." Carmen Dell'Orefice
wears a strapless corselet. The
model, famous now for her striking
white hair and remarkably youthful
beauty, continued to work until she
was in her eighties.

↑ There's a suburban feel to this April 2017 story "Good Housekeeping", which marries the tropes of old-style femininity with lounge-around streetwear, both key trends for that Spring/Summer. Jane How styles an elegant Olivier Theyskens white lace corset with Lacoste tracksuit trousers.

→ Yasmeen Ghauri smoulders in a John Galliano white tulle dress with a corset top in this May 1992 image. On graduating from London's Saint Martin's School of Art in 1984, Galliano's final collection – "Les Incroyables" – caught the attention of the fashion elite. "There was this incredible attention to detail," fashion commentator Caryn Franklin told *Vogue*. "Painstaking storytelling and unashamed enjoyment of the past."

← An important piece of fashion history is revealed in the October 1947 issue: the taffeta underbodice with rose-ruffles at the breasts and a ruffled hip, designed by Christian Dior as the foundation for his New Look Autumn 1947 Paris collection. As *Vogue* commented: "There are moments when fashion changes fundamentally. When it is more than a matter of differences in detail. The whole fashion attitude seems to change – the whole structure of the body. This is one of those moments...It all began when the word 'femininity' crept back at the war's end. For femininity implies a figure, and you certainly need a figure – your own, or an aided effort – to wear the clothes we show in this issue..."

↑ A June 2006 feature entitled "Burlesque" welcomed the return of the corset. "Enter the captivating world of shapely bodices, boudoir frills and showgirl sparkle." Here, Guinevere van Seenus wears a silk corset embroidered with feathers and sequins, by Rossella Tarabini for Anna Molinari, and Agent Provocateur fishnet hold-ups.

↑ With her womanly figure and simmering sex appeal, model Lara Stone has transformed the fashion landscape. In the eponymous story "Stone Age" from December 2009, she conjures the look of a Hollywood screen siren of the Fifties in Dior's haute couture embroidered silk-faille and lace corset dress.

→ In a punkily nostalgic ripped bodice and tartan kilt, Rosemary Ferguson incites a bit of fashion anarchy in a January 2002 story called "The Morning after the Year Before…". Her leather corset, adorned with a dismembered doll, was created for the London boutique The Pineal Eye by Vava Dudu with Fabrice Lorrain. A stylist and artist who designed corsets for Jean Paul Gaultier and outfits for Lady Gaga, Dudu shuns newness and brands and logos, believing instead in repurposing and customizing used clothing.

← "From waist-cinching corsets to subtle tailoring, the hourglass silhouette makes a comeback." In July 2001, Alexander McQueen gave the bustier a light touch for Givenchy with his cotton tulle design and a matching sequinned skirt. For some of his more theatrical creations, McQueen worked with the legendary corsetière Mr Pearl, who is as well known for his work with designers such as Thierry Mugler, Jean Paul Gaultier and John Galliano as he is for his own commitment to wearing corsets night and day to maintain his 46cm (18in) waist.

↑ The gilt chain armlets worn with Valentino's lustrous gold silk brocade bustier lend a gladiatorial air to this image from March 1990, yet the first recorded corsets preceded even classical civilization – they were worn by the Bronze Age Minoans in Crete. Both men and women had form-fitting vests and belts to constrict and shape the waist. Ancient Greek women wore an elaborate girdle called a zona, to shape the waist and support the breasts. It was Catherine de Medici who introduced the corset as an undergarment to the French court in the 1500s.

↑ For a playful story in the April 2007 issue, *Vogue*'s Charlotte Stockdale, a team of her colleagues and students from Central Saint Martin's, London, created exquisite handmade paper dresses to set off the season's statement accessories of towering platforms and power bags. This corset was made from old *Vogue* sewing patterns and the voluminous skirt was crafted from khadi-pulp paper.

→ Versace's body-sculpting superwoman suit embroidered with Swarovski crystals demands epic poise from Kate Moss in June 2012. The idea of the corset as a stylized and moulded protective carapace took hold in the late 20th century, when Jean Paul Gaultier and Thierry Mugler's exaggerated interpretations could transform the wearer into an Amazon, biker or robot. Some critics considered their corsets an assault against the model's body, while others viewed them as elevating the female form to something almost beyond human.

← Bra tops were a recurring theme
for Spring 2017, as seen in this
example by Céline in the February
2017 issue. A cotton bustier worn
over the top of it with slouchy
trousers was, according to *Vogue*,
"a clever combination that replaces
the slip dress now".

↑ "Master the new high-low mix;
seductive underwear speeds
trusty sportswear into the next
season to create wardrobe
champions." Was this a new
iteration of the corset? In the
feature entitled "Earth Angel"
from the May 2016 issue, the
magazine proposed: "Invest in
luxurious staples that borrow
the contouring lines of classic
underwear." Considered a new-
season essential, the structured

linen/cotton body is worn here
with a cotton/silk bumbag (fanny
pack), both by Balenciaga.

↑ In "Couture Stripped" in May 2006, Lucinda Chambers casts aside Givenchy's sumptuous scarlet gown to reveal a glimpse of the panoply of underpinnings worn by model Freja Beha Erichsen: a Givenchy silk-tulle and cotton underskirt, a cotton-poplin bra from Passionbait.com and a white denim corset by Miki Fukai at The Pineal Eye. The image perhaps obliquely references Horst P Horst's 1939 classic black-and white photograph of the shadowed back view of a woman laced into a Mainbocher corset.

→ In its "New Modern" feature from February 2013, *Vogue* declared that "Fashion is in a new mood – modern and minimal, yes, but devoutly feminine, grown-up and oh so seductive." Romance and passion combine in the Rochas blush-coloured conical bustier and the Michael Kors fiery red jacket. The conical bra cups reference the Fifties cone style and Madonna's stagewear, designed by Jean Paul Gaultier, that she wore on her 1990 Blond Ambition tour.

← There was "a magpie approach to dress", reported *Vogue* in its "Modern British" feature from February 1985 about the London Spring Collections. British designers took cloth out of its usual context and focused on texture and pattern, while playing with rich colour, embroidery and brocade. This brocade corset, laced up with silky rope, and a suspender skirt, worn together over a cropped, cotton jersey T-shirt and a miniskirt, all by Claire Sharp, spoke to the eccentric punk inventiveness of British designers in the mid-Eighties.

↑ "Lady lace gets all shook up with sugar-almond shades, brothel creepers and arch-browed attitude; wear day or night." In the "More Dash Than Cash" story from January 2010, 25 years on from the image opposite, there is another eclectic mix of a lace top and vintage petticoat, this time pulled together by a silk-mix bustier from Asos.com.

↑ Grand couture evening wear was the focus of October 1997's "Opulence" story. Models Karen Elson and Eden Rountree strike elegant poses "fit for a Sargent portrait" in *belle-époque*-inspired gowns by John Galliano for Christian Dior. With back-laced corset bodices, the dresses are made of sumptuous lace and patterned silks, inspired by Egypt and English flower gardens, and adorned with masses of glistering jet. Renowned for his visionary collections based on extraordinarily diverse historical and geographical influences, Galliano has often incorporated both hard and soft lingerie details into his work for Dior, Maison Martin Margiela and his eponymous line.

→ A January 1954 feature, entitled "Beauty partners Fashion", highlights how clothing (and therefore lingerie) can throw new emphasis on a part of the body previously unrevealed, and the importance of one's beauty regime.

"Growing late-day fashion – the dress with a waist-deep V at back, high neck at front, which makes specialized demands: a bare-backed bra, a corset to nip the waist neatly, and back complexion treatment as careful as you'd give to your face." Here, a model in a made-to-measure waist-nipper by the corsetière Illa Knina, combining corset, bare-backed bra and petticoat with a rounded skirt line, buffs her shoulder to achieve the perfect finish.

← Naomi Campbell appears in the June 1995 "Beauty and the Basque" feature in this peppermint lace-back corset with hook-and-eye front fastening, by Gianfranco Ferré. *Vogue* notes, "Fashion has rediscovered the beauty of curves. The current mood of nostalgia has inspired designers to take a fresh look at the age-old art of corsetry. The laces, hooks and eyes live on in this new breed of basques and bustiers but the use of modern stretch fabrics results in pieces that are more dynamic than period, more Superwoman than saloon showgirl." June Kenton of the British lingerie label Rigby & Peller told the magazine, "Nowadays, we fit our corsets to the wearer; not the wearer to them." As a result, *Vogue* pointed out, while they won't give you a 19in waist, nor will they give you bulges above and below. These corsets are about smoothing and shaping, not cinching and puckering.

↑ This still-life from November 1993 features an exquisite bustier made for the Autumn/Winter couture collection by Christian Lacroix – a strapless silk velvet and embroidered gold lamé bodice sculpted to fit over the waist and hips. The caption reads, "Modern couture is still the story of exquisite artistry. But now, it's also a tale of the unexpected; of wit, daring and impish irreverence."

↑ Recumbent on a sofa, Malgosia Bela smoulders like a Cinecittà heroine in Dolce & Gabbana's glorious organza lace-up crinoline bustier dress and a What Katie Did satin bra for the April 2009 issue. The Polish model later told *Vogue*, "When I choose lingerie, I think about who is going to wear it – or who is going to take it off, actually, if the evening goes well. It's the balance between feeling extremely seductive and sexy, and also being comfortable, being at peace with yourself."

→ Dolce & Gabbana again but in a completely different mood from the image above, this time giving a quietly seductive flavour to elegant tailoring. For this October 2003 feature, Charlotte Pilcher subtly plays with propriety by juxtaposing classic components of smart daywear – a wool jacket, trousers and discreet gold jewellery – with a quilted satin corset. The model's leather-gloved hand on her waist, anchoring the jacket open and thereby revealing the corset and décolleté, adds an extra frisson to the picture.

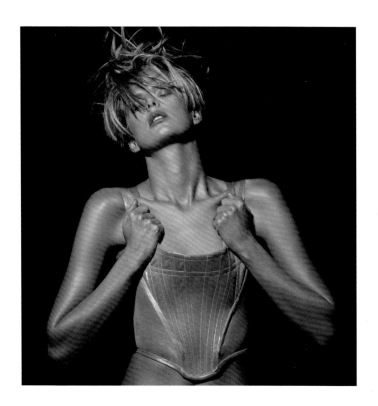

← In June 2007, 60 years after Christian Dior's New Look collection, Harriet Quick reported that John Galliano celebrated a triumphant decade as head of design at Dior by re-creating the iconic silhouette with his own inimitable touch. Canadian model Daria Werbowy wears a silk corset, the garment that has always given the Dior woman her perfect hourglass shape. "I wanted to show people that it was time to return to glamour," said Galliano of the collection. "Being bashful is so last season."

↑ Featured in the September 1989 issue, this shimmering gold ciré Liberty bodice by Vivienne Westwood was very definitely intended as a piece of outerwear. Liberty bodices were invented at the end of the 19th century as an alternative to the strictures of traditional corsets. Often made of warm, fleecy fabric, they had no boning, and there were buttons at the waist to which elastic tapes for stockings could be attached. They were worn by women and girls, for whom it was thought they would provide warmth and some

support in maintaining a good posture. Some older women in the UK wore Liberty bodices until as recently as the Seventies.

after dark

Sex. In any discussion of lingerie it's never far away. The two have been an item since way back. After all, one invariably leads to the other: a little black lace, some slinky satin, fishnet stockings, a feather here, a nipple tassel there...

"It would be disingenuous to pretend that lingerie photographs haven't often been regarded, at least in part, as tasteful, high-class porn," said *Vogue* in November 1995. With sensuous fabrics and tantalizing transparency offering peekaboo glimpses of the body's most erogenous areas, lingerie can be powerfully seductive.

Few would argue that a partially clothed body isn't sexier than a nude one. In his famous essay "Striptease", from his 1957 book *Mythologies,* philosopher Roland Barthes wrote of "the eroticism of the partially hidden body". Lingerie exists in a secret realm between our bodies and our clothes, touching the most intimate parts of us. It's to some extent this combination of mystery and promise of sex that imbues it with an erotic charge, but also the myriad gendered experiences brought to it by the wearer, for whom it is worn and, in the case of a magazine, the team behind the photograph.

Historically, the British weren't renowned for being very racy in the lingerie department, a reputation probably rooted in the stiff-upper-lip reserve of the national DNA, epitomized by a preoccupation with wearing undergarments sufficiently presentable so as not to offend a policeman or a paramedic if you were involved in an accident. Fortunately, things have moved on.

A pioneer of seductive, romantic underwear, Janet Reger began her lingerie business because she felt that, while fashion in the late

← The "Kate's World" fashion shoot from December 2014 was testament to Kate Moss's extraordinary versatility and longevity as a model, almost 20 years after she first appeared in the contentious "heroin-chic" story in June 1993 (see page 59). Here, she is the embodiment of a Sixties sex kitten. With her hand resting on a leopardskin coat (Hello, Mrs Robinson!), she's all legs, lace and lips in a La Perla body, black stilettos and backcombed Bardot hair. Voilà! The cat's meow.

Sixties may have been swinging, it wasn't sensuous, and although women did buy and wear vintage dresses, she couldn't find lingerie to channel the old-school Hollywood glamour she recalled seeing in her mother's wardrobe. By the mid-Seventies, the name Janet Reger conjured sex and glamour. Joan Collins and David Bowie were among the brand's fans, and further cultural recognition came when it appeared in a 1976 Tom Stoppard play, *Dirty Linen*, worn, rather appropriately, by the character Miss Gotobed. Today, brands such as Coco de Mer and Myla purvey tasteful lingerie and erotica from boudoir-like London boutiques or from online.

By the end of the 20th century, sex was everywhere, in fashion, music, advertising and the burgeoning pornography industry. From Madonna's controversial *Sex* book of 1992 to explicit scenes in films such as *Basic Instinct,* released the same year, sex sold, or at least provoked a conversation.

Fashion loved it. Domenico Dolce & Stefano Gabbana were among the greatest exponents, tapping the archetype of a voluptuous Sicilian woman based on the va-va-voom silhouettes of Fifties film stars. Cleverly fusing the symbolism of the maternal and the passionate, the designers reworked classic black slips into dresses that pushed up the breasts and emphasized the hips. Bra tops, black lace and bustiers were often tantalizingly visible beneath. At the same time, the Wonderbra lifted breasts literally and metaphorically. Discovered in 1992 by fashion insiders as a way to "get the look" of a cleavage without undergoing cosmetic surgery, the Wonderbra was described by *Vogue* as a cult classic.

Themes of bondage and fetishism appeared on the catwalks. "Miss S&M" (Gianni Versace's Autumn/Winter 1992 collection) took elements such as buckles, straps, chains and black leather from the dungeon to the red carpet in glamorous evening wear. Although outwardly androgynous and functional, Helmut Lang's sharp, minimalist designs, the beloved uniform of a tribe of fashion editors, surreptitiously included bondage harnesses, trash bags, bra straps and rubber.

The mid-Nineties was an opportune time for Vivienne Westwood's son Joseph Corré and his then wife Serena Rees to open Agent Provocateur in London's Soho, selling provocative designer underwear for women. As much about sex as it was about foundation garments – they sold whips alongside knickers – it was a huge success. Corré told *Vogue* in June 1996 how quickly his customers became hooked. "It's a bit like a drug," he said. "Women come in here and start off by buying one or two pieces. Then they get home, wear them and can't believe it. They look at themselves in a different way. They're on a buzz and they have to have more." The store was famous for its service, and the staff uniform – a short pink nurse's style shirtdress and black stockings – became instantly recognizable as code for what *Guardian* journalist Eva Wiseman, a former employee, described as "kink luxe".

The television series *Sex and the City* (1998–2004) became a cultural landmark for many reasons, one of which was the pivotal sartorial role played by the characters' lingerie. "It changed the way women thought about their underwear," said Myla co-founder Charlotte Semler in the *Guardian* in January 2004. "It became a cool part of fashion – you saw these beautiful, highly styled women and half the time they were in their bra and pants. And it wasn't 'tarts in the boudoir' underwear or M&S, it was beautiful in the way Jimmy Choo shoes or a Dior handbag are beautiful."

In some ways, the high-octane sexiness and provocative imagery of Tom Ford's advertising campaigns for Gucci and Yves Saint Laurent were the high-gloss antithesis of this "realness", although causing no less controversy. Particularly notable were the images of a Gucci "G" shaved into model Carmen Kass's pubic hair in 2003, and a naked Sophie Dahl in 2000, erotically supine on black silk for the Opium fragrance campaign. Complaints that the images were too sexually suggestive resulted in them both being banned from billboards, although not from magazines.

It is interesting in a #MeToo era, in which sexual harassment allegations have been made against a number of the world's leading fashion photographers, to consider by whom, on whom and for whom lingerie is photographed. Will the collective vision of the growing number of female fashion photographers supplant the Seventies conceit of the male gaze with a female gaze?

It's important to remember, too, that while the sense of confidence and power many women feel in wearing sexy lingerie heightens their appeal to men, it is not necessarily their sole intention. As this book attempts to explain, lingerie is a fashion essential – symbolic and psychologically rich for all the meanings it conveys. Above all, it is the element of self-spoiling sensuality that lingerie promises. As Sarah Mower pointed out in June 1988, "a woman may enjoy luxurious underwear solely for her own pleasure" with a "sensibility which derives sensual and aesthetic pleasures from tactile, beautifully crafted things".

↑ Sensual and titillating, feathers have long been associated with the boudoir. In this image from December 1974, they conjure images of Vegas showgirls and Hollywood movie stars (think Gloria Swanson, Jean Harlow, Marilyn Monroe) as the model lounges in a cream satin peignoir edged in pink marabou. A long outer garment frequently made of sheer fabric, the peignoir gets its name from the French word *peigner*, meaning "to comb", to describe a garment worn while brushing one's hair.

→ "Shield your eyes from the sumptuousness of Valentino's sparkling silk," teases the caption to this "Couture Stripped" story from May 2006. The sensuousness of the fabric is almost palpable – the model appears in a reverie, her eyes closed behind the veil, hand covering her breast as the dress's strap falls from her shoulder.

→ → The caption for this August 1991 feature reads, "Every rising starlet knows the career value of what she puts next to her pampered skin. White satin, lace, marabou, underwiring – this girl will stop at nothing." Draped across the bed, fingers through her thick, glossy hair, Stephanie Seymour puts in an award-worthy performance of seduction. A lingerie and hosiery model for Victoria's Secret in its early days, Seymour launched her own lingerie line, Raven & Sparrow, in 2017.

← "Attention please, this bra works wonders," announced Sarah Mower in the December 1991 issue. She described the Wonderbra as, "A masterpiece of engineering... underwired and deeply plunged, with a bow nesting between the cups, patented 'gate-back' for unsurpassed lift and covering of dense, opaque lace: ergo eminently suitable for outerwear or glimpsed as a subtle flash."

↑ Peeping through an open door in this September 1967 story, we glimpse a girl wearing a pretty plunging black bra by Goddard with bikini briefs from Peter Pan: "beautiful black lace, nothing less. And nothing more alluring now for undercover fashion."

↑ "Where to draw the line between under- and outerwear?" is the question posed in this "Love on the Left Bank" story for October 2015. Kate Moss as fashion editor styles Lara Stone in a lace dress with gold chain detail by Alessandra Rich, revealing a sliver of her inner thigh above black stockings worn with Dolce & Gabbana slingback stilettos. *Vogue*'s claim exactly 50 years earlier in October 1965 that, "Black lace always has, always will, look romantic, feminine, seductive," certainly holds true.

→ More black lace is featured in the "Belle de Nuit" fashion shoot from September 2005. The minute floral detail on the Alessandro Dell'Acqua dress etches a delicate veil over the body of model Behati Prinsloo. The soft black bow falling off her shoulder, revealing the strap of the Agent Provocateur bra, her up/down hairstyle and the slight blush to her cheeks suggest a certain seductive dishevelment. Dell'Acqua's signature style is based on the fragile interplay of chiffon pieces and lingerie. Known

for an eroticized elegance, his clothes often layer translucent blacks, beiges and nude chiffons that evoke lingerie.

← The keyhole frame of this September 2005 image introduces a layer of secrecy, calling into question whether the model is aware of our gaze and heightening the position of the reader as voyeur. Gemma Ward wears a silk-chiffon shirtdress with lace inserts by Valentino Boutique and an Agent Provocateur underslip, highlighting the boudoir trend in the Autumn collections of that year.

↑ Sasha Pivovarova wears Yves Saint Laurent's wool tuxedo dress in the September 2007 issue. The iconic French designer gave menswear-inspired styling a huge shot of sex appeal with his Le Smoking tuxedo in 1966, which was hailed as the alternative to the Little Black Dress. Here, tailored to fit feminine curves and worn with black stockings, Louboutin heels and a knowing expression, his dress is loaded with sexual ambiguity. And is she undoing or doing up her suspenders?

→ → According to *Vogue* in March 2006, "whether she's modelling ready-to-wear or underwear, Kate Moss is pure pin-up". Here, she wears a Passion Bait silk bra and knickers by designer Janine Rose, whose underwear collections were inspired by the delicate, long-forgotten details of Fifties and Sixties French lingerie and stocking-lingerie fetishes. "The sex kitten purrs in steely silk lingerie and coquettish pull-ups."

↑ The painterly light, soft and slightly hazy in this November 1990 image, casts the model into an intimate semi-darkness and imbues her ivory satin Rosy bra with a pearly luminosity, reminiscent of white flowers in the gloaming. The effect heightens our sense of the sumptuousness of the fabrics she wears – the gentle weight of the softest Perry Ellis cashmere wrap and the cool smoothness of the slippery satin.

→ In this image from September 2005, come-to-bed eyes, kissed-clean lips and big-tease hair hark back to Brigitte Bardot and the Sixties. With her coat thrown over her shoulders, a gentle arch in her back and her top half slightly twisted, the model subtly pushes her bust forward to make her invitation clear. The silk and lace bra by Nina Ricci, and the Agent Provocateur briefs, suspender belt and stockings do the rest.

"Mixing sophistication with undeniable sex appeal, grown-up glamour just got a whole lot more interesting." So says *Vogue* in its September 2002 feature "How Do You Want Me?" Missy Rayder, whose sister Frankie appears opposite, unbuttons her Chanel suit to reveal a Passion Bait silk-satin bra and lace knickers.

← "Ruffle his feathers by wearing Valentino's sexy chiffon blouse," reads the caption to this September 2003 image, styled by Charlotte Pilcher. Frankie Rayder lies back in coquettish deshabille, in a floaty layered skirt and barely-there feather-trimmed chiffon blouse, temptingly unbuttoned to reveal Gucci's tulle underwired bra. The skirt is pulled up to reveal a suspender belt playfully printed onto her tights.

↑ Lingerie codes translate to evening wear in this image from the January 2003 shoot "Pillow Talk", with a Philosophy di Alberta Ferretti navy satin minidress, with velvet detailing, worn with a pink satin camisole. The model is Natalia Vodianova, nicknamed "Supernova" and known for her rags-to-riches story and philanthropic endeavours. In 2016 she made her fifth appearance in the Pirelli Calendar.

↑ Twiggy appears "as a saucy flapper" in this December 1974 image. With a nod to the Roaring Twenties, when shorter dress lengths revealed women's legs for the first time, Twiggy coyly rests her chin on her hand as she slides up the hem of her beaded drop-waist dress to reveal a titillating black lace garter on her black Wolford tights.

→ "Ooh la la! Wickedly sexy black lace lingerie," exclaims the caption to this May 1992 image. The performative power of lingerie is evident in the suggestive moves of the model as she puts on a cabaret-style show in a black lace underwired bra by Playtex, tulle gloves by Christian Lacroix, La Perla lace knickers and sheer tights by Pretty Polly. Playtex, an American company founded in 1947, derives its name from a fusion of the words "play" and "latex". It was behind two of the most famous items of women's underwear: the Cross Your Heart bra of the Fifties and the 18-Hour Girdle of the Sixties.

← In the "Red Hot Black Leather" story from January 1992, Yasmeen Ghauri combines downtown attitude with uptown chic. *Vogue* opined that the sexiest way to wear leather was with fishnet, patent and lace. The grid-patterned tights draw attention to her legs, the lacy push-up La Perla to her cleavage, the biker boots and leather jacket add a tough edge, while the shiny skirt and quilted choker suggest a touch of the dominatrix.

↑ This photograph from March 2014 was styled by Kate Moss, who took as her inspiration Niagara, the lead vocalist of the influential late Seventies Detroit proto-punk band Destroy All Monsters. Model Daria Werbowy wears Azzedine Alaïa's bra top and grommet-strewn miniskirt, both in black leather, suggesting an anarchic twist. Artist as well as musician, Niagara produced flyers and album art for the band and

became known for her depictions of tough, gorgeous women with a dangerous demeanour, which were inspired by comic strips.

↑ The March 2001 issue presented a bondage theme: "straps, buckles and all things shiny and black are the key to this season's hard-edged accessories". Helmut Lang's stretch silk creation with multiple straps on the back provides the perfect backdrop for a range of accessories. These include a leather fingerless glove by Hermes and multistrap leather sandals from Patrick Cox.

→ Eighties themes of sex and power are visited here in February 2001 in Helmut Lang's sophisticated take on the leather bondage dress and matching bra. The crossing straps and cut-outs give the look a sexual charge by both covering and revealing the body at the same time.

← In the September 2003 issue, the combination of the disparate textures of animal fur, leather and a chunky metal chain with Costume National's black wool hook-and-eye corset, Calvin Klein's black mesh underwired bra and hipster shorts and thigh-high boots by Givenchy makes for a fetishist's delight.

↑ Also from September 2003, the opaque collar and cuffs of Givenchy designer Julien Macdonald's otherwise sheer silk polo-neck top draw attention to the model's neck and wrists, a subtle reference to slave symbolism, a motif in private bondage and occasionally seen on the catwalk. Thigh-high boots, considered by many to be erotic and often worn by dominatrices, are an occasional fashion trend.

→ → "Cheat your way to an hourglass silhouette in Antonio Berardi's body-contouring corseted dress," coaxes the caption to this image from the April 2010 story inspired by Tina Turner's 1984 album *Private Dancer*. "Consider this a masterclass in seduction," says *Vogue*.

↑ Guinevere van Seenus celebrates the timeless allure of showgirls in September 2009, with inspiration taken from the seductive art of burlesque and the dramatic beauty of theatrical make-up. Her cupless bodice is from Trashy Lingerie, a private LA store patronized by as many Hollywood A-listers as you can think of – its slogan is "Our Fantasy Is Fulfilling Yours". The nipple tassels and fingerless gloves are from Atsuko Kudo, a London-based designer who has pioneered the use of latex as a couture fabric, working with Hussein Chalayan, Vivienne Westwood and Riccardo Tisci. Her designs have been worn by Beyoncé, Dita Von Teese and Grace Jones.

→ "We are in love with breasts," Stefano Gabbana of Dolce & Gabbana told *Vogue* in August 2001. "They embody a sweet feeling, like maternity, but at the same time they are a symbol of passion. That's why we love to celebrate them – with a bra strap that can be seen, or a bra you can see through a sheer shirt." In this November 2007 image, the Dolce & Gabbana silk bra is worn with an ostrich-feather cape by Basia Zarzycka and stockings by Agent Provocateur. "Stockings and heels, a flash of leopard-print and a shake of feathers make the perfect costume," states the caption.

← "Remember the golden age of cabaret and bring out your inner starlet with shimmering eyes and pouting lips," advises *Vogue* in the June 2008 story "Stardust Memories". Canadian model Jessica Stam wears La Perla stockings, sequinned shorts from Les Chiffoniers and a silk bra from Damaris for Roksanda Ilincic. The two designers collaborated on a range of underwear for the Spring/Summer 2008 season. "The goal was to create a dreamy and ethereal atmosphere, infused with a little bit of unexpected surprise," Roksanda told Vogue.co.uk in March 2009.

↑ "Welcome to the return of the corset. Enter the captivating world of shapely bodices, boudoir frills and showgirl sparkle," says *Vogue* in the "Burlesque" story from June 2006. Godmother of burlesque Gypsy Rose Lee, credited with inventing the art of the striptease in the Thirties, never appeared naked in public. She knew that the sexy persona she had developed relied on parts of her body being covered – that the illusion of her nakedness was far more sensual than the sight of her bare flesh. Here, Guinevere van Seenus entices in a Jean Paul Gaultier silk blouse, a Lycra-mix body from Liza Bruce and hold-ups from Wolford.

↑ Featured in the 1 April 1979 issue, the "Dress for the Late Night Life" shoot was photographed in the Pavilion at The Dorchester, London, a suite of intimate, mid-century, baroque-fantasy party rooms, designed by Oliver Messel. The model wears a glossy black body by the German corset company Silhouette, a spotted black net camisole-slip by Shuji Tojo, flocked milliner's net from John Lewis and black suede sandals by Maud Frizon.

→ The buckles down the front of the high-cut leather corset by Belt Lady, the long leather gloves and the rubber bangles worn around the model's ankles give a fetishistic air to this image from "Superheroines of the Black and Silver Screens", in the October 1984 issue.

← Eva Herzigova reclines in a black stretch lace, high-necked body by Triumph, ultra-sheer tights by Aristoc and Jimmy Choo heels, for this May 1992 shoot. The Folies Bergère poster recalls the Parisian cabaret music hall, which opened in 1869. Its famous risqué revues featured extravagant costumes and sets, and launched the career of Josephine Baker, whose most sensational costume consisted only of a girdle of bananas.

↑ "Our showgirl, Kate Moss, knows all the secrets to seduction: sequins, corsets and perfectly made-up eyes, lips and nails," declared *Vogue* in October 2013. Here she wears a bra from Fifi Chachnil and Prada's jewelled knickers. The gold corset is by Sian Hoffman, a London "artisan" corsetière who has reshaped the traditional corset to fit a more modern ideal, but still includes at least 12 steel bones in each one.

→ → There is an atmosphere of film noir – the natural habitat of the femme fatale – about this image from the story "No Smoke without Fire", from November 2004. The low lighting, stark shadows and wide-angle shot are typical of the genre. A woman stands in a cocktail dress, bra revealed and finished with Swarovski-crystal brooches – all from Valentino Boutique – looking at someone or something we can't see.

↑ For the November 2018 issue, singer-songwriter Taylor Swift wears a taffeta and lace bra top and skirt with sheer panels from Alexander McQueen, styled by *Vogue* Editor-in-Chief Edward Enninful. Her pencil-thin eyebrows and waved hair are worn flat against her head, recalling a Twenties flapper girl.

→ "Louche lounging: making the transition from night, the dressing gown and suspender belt trip into day," was how *Vogue* described this image of model Nina Brosh in a lace suspender belt by Gossard and Wolford stockings beneath a Yohji Yamamoto kimono dressing gown. For this October 1994 "Madam Butterfly" story, the magazine stated that, "Artifice and glamour, the age-old tools of the courtesan, fill evenings with a heavy decadence. Designers open up an erotic past of black lacquer satins, cherry red kimonos and opulent cheongsams, crowned by headdresses of exotic silk flowers." The year before this shoot, Brosh appeared in the video for Duran Duran's version of The Velvet Underground's "Femme Fatale".

← "Challenging what works for the body now, designers have restructured underwear as outerwear. Bodysuits, corsets and lingerie emerge newly minted"– so said *Vogue* in February 1991. Helena Christensen looks athletically sexy in Fendi's satin and lycra girdled body and Wolford's lace-top hold-ups. The term "hold-ups" was first used by Pretty Polly in 1967 for its self-supporting stockings. As skirts got shorter, hold-ups fell out of favour, prompting the rise in the popularity of tights.

↑ The camera's angle focuses the reader's eye unambiguously on the La Perla lace bra worn underneath the model's jacket in "Under Cover", from November 1988. Her masculine shoulder-padded power suit – the dress code for professional women in the Eighties – contrasts noticeably with the overt femininity of the fragile tracery of the lace bra and her loose updo (which looks as though it may tumble seductively around her shoulders with the slightest encouragement).

→ → Kate Moss as fashion editor styles a pitch-perfect take on classic Parisian seduction in October 2015. "Chanel's doily-collar jacket whispers of a maid's uniform. Step up the seduction with suspenders and T-bar shoes with lipstick-red sole," commented *Vogue*. The submissive propriety of the top half of the look is subverted by the overt sexuality of Lara Stone's provocatively turned hips, revealing her La Perla suspender knickers and Agent Provocateur stockings.

↑ In the September 1991 story "High Drama", *Vogue* describes how "all the exotic riches of a movie heroine's wardrobe have made a big entrance in winter fashion". Ready for her close-up, Tatjana Patitz as screen siren cuts a lone figure on the beach, draped in Dolce & Gabbana's faux leopardskin evening coat over her scarlet silk corset and fishnet tights.

→ Adopting a pin-up girl pose, Kate Moss, the ultimate poster girl, casts a backward glance in the April 2010 story "Basic Instinct". She wears a silk bra by The Lake & Stars, a miniskirt of sheared silk tufts by Moschino, seamed tights by Pamela Mann and patent leather heels by Christian Louboutin. Pin-up imagery dates to the end of the 19th century, when burlesque performers and actresses began to use photographic advertisements as business cards to promote themselves. At the same time, American artist Charles Gibson's illustrations of a feminine ideal of physical attractiveness – known as the "Gibson Girls" – caught the public's imagination and could be cut out of the magazine and newspapers in which they appeared and "pinned up" on a wall. The idea of using images of women in varying degrees of undress to sell things has been co-opted many times since: as sexy patriots on wartime propaganda posters, the Vargas magazine girls of the Forties, in Madison Avenue advertising campaigns in the Fifties and Sixties, and as Hugh Hefner's muses for *Playboy* magazine.

index

Glossary for British/North American terms

handbag	purse/pocketbook
knickers	panties
pants	panties
pinafore	jumper dress
suspenders	garters
tights	pantyhose
tracksuit	sweatsuit
trousers	pants

acknowledgements

An Hachette UK Company
www.hachette.co.uk

First published in Great Britain in 2019 by
Conran Octopus Ltd,
a division of Octopus Publishing Group Ltd
Carmelite House, 50 Victoria Embankment
London EC4Y 0DZ
www.octopusbooks.co.uk
www.octopusbooksusa.com

Text copyright © The Condé Nast
Publications Ltd 2019

Design & layout copyright © Octopus
Publishing Group Ltd 2019

Distributed in the US by Hachette Book Group,
1290 Avenue of the Americas, 4th and 5th
Floors, New York, NY 10104

Distributed in Canada by Canadian Manda
Group, 664 Annette St., Toronto, Ontario,
Canada M6S 2C8

VOGUE registered trademark is owned
by The Condé Nast Publications Limited
and is used under licence from it. All rights
reserved.

All rights reserved. No part of this work
may be reproduced or utilized in any form
or by any means, electronic or mechanical,
including photocopying, recording or by
any information storage and retrieval
system, without the prior written
permission of the publisher.

The Right of The Condé Nast Publications
Ltd to be identified as the author of this Work
has been asserted in accordance with the
Copyright, Designs and Patents Act 1988.

ISBN 978 1 84091 768 0

A CIP catalogue record for this book
is available from the British Library.

Printed and bound in China

10 9 8 7 6 5 4 3 2 1

Publisher: Alison Starling
Creative Director: Jonathan Christie
Junior Editor: Ella Parsons
Copy Editor: Helen Ridge
Production Controller: Emily Noto

Special thanks to Harriet Wilson, Carole
Dumoulin, Agnes Bataclan, Viktorija
Berlickaite, Frith Carlisle and Poppy Roy
at The Condé Nast Publications Ltd.

Every effort has been made to reproduce
the colours in this book accurately;
however, the printing process can lead
to some discrepancies.

Unless otherwise stated, all text and
photographs are taken from British *Vogue*.

Photography credits:

Front cover Antony Denney; back cover
Sante D'Orazio; 2 Claude Virgin; 4 Tim
Walker; 7 Philip Castle; 8 Mario Testino; 10
Nick Knight; 11 Alasdair McLellan; 13 Herb
Ritts; 14 Andrew Macpherson; 18 Anthony
Gilbert; 19 Bobby Hilson; 20 Neil Kirk; 21 Clive
Arrowsmith; 22 Michael English; 23 Harry
Peccinotti; 24 Just Jaeckin; 25 © Norman
Parkinson/Iconic Images; 26 Glen Luchford;
27 Daniel Jackson; 28 Collier Schorr; 29 Nick
Knight; 30–31 Tessa Traeger; 32 Guy Bourdin;
33 Helmut Newton; 34 Hans Feurer;
35 Alasdair McLellan; 36 Alasdair McLellan;
37 Alasdair McLellan; 38 Steven Klein; 39
Raymond Meier; 40 Patrick Demarchelier;
44 Craig McDean; 45 Paolo Roversi;
46 Antonio; 47 Sante D'Orazio; 48 Juergen
Teller; 49 Albert Watson; 50–51 Mario
Testino; 52 Eric Boman; 53 David Bailey;
54 Dennis Davidson; 55 Robin Derrick;
56 Peter Knapp; 57 Sante D'Orazio; 58 Paolo
Roversi; 59 Corinne Day; 60–61 Patrick
Demarchelier; 62 Barry Lategan; 63 Vanina
Sorrenti; 64 Alex Chatelain; 65 Norbert
Schoerner; 66–67 Mario Testino; 68 John
Stember; 69 Eamonn McCabe; 70 Juergen
Teller; 71 Tyrone Lebon; 72 Neil Kirk;
73 Mikael Jansson; 74 Raymond Meier;
78 Nick Knight; 79 Ellen Von Unwerth;
80 Peter Lindbergh; 81 Dennis Davidson;
82–83 © Norman Parkinson/Iconic Images;
84 Glen Luchford; 85 Herb Ritts; 86 Clifford
Coffin; 87 Craig McDean; 88 Mario Testino;
89 Corinne Day; 90 Raymond Meier;
91 Steven Klein; 92 Lachley Bailey; 93 Mert
Alas & Marcus Piggott; 94 Zoe Ghertner;
95 Harley Weir; 96 Javier Vallhonrat;
97 Patrick Demarchelier; 98 Kim Knott;
99 Ami Sioux; 100 Arthur Elgort; 101 Anthony
Denney; 102 Nick Knight; 103 Albert Watson;
104 Javier Vallhonrat; 105 Robert Watts;
106 Paolo Roversi; 107 Steven Klein; 108
Mario Testino; 112 Eric Boman; 113 Javier

Vallhonrat; 114–115 Sante D'Orazio;
116 Andrea Blanchi; 117 © Norman
Parkinson/Iconic Images; 118 Inez &
Vinoodh; 119 Paolo Roversi; 120 Nick Knight;
121 Corinne Day; 122–123 Nick Knight;
124 Sheila Metzner; 125 Paolo Roversi;
126–127 Mario Testino; 128 Raymond Meier;
129 Karen Collins; 130 Barry Lategan;
131 Ellen Von Unwerth; 132 Sante D'Orazio;
133 Mert Alas & Marcus Piggott; 134 Lee
Jenkins; 135 Tom Munro; 136 Mark & Sam;
137 Norbert Schoerner; 138–139 Javier
Vallhonrat; 140 Paolo Roversi; 141 Paolo
Roversi; 142 Patrick Demarchelier;
143 Craig McDean; 144 Joe Gaffney;
145 Albert Watson; 146 Ellen Von Unwerth;
147 Javier Vallhonrat; 148–149 Laurie
Bartley; 150 Mert Alas & Marcus Piggott; 151
Pamela Hanson; 152 Herb Ritts; 153 William
Garrett; 154–155 Inez & Vinoodh; 156 Peter
Lindbergh; 157 Willy Vanderperre.

Page 2: For this November 1961 photograph,
the model wears a bitter chocolate brown
slip by Taylor-Woods, made of the fabric
Bri-nylon. A deep trimming of ecru lace is
carefully shaped around the bust and falls
from the hem.

Page 4: Riffing on the magical world of
Roald Dahl, this whimsical shoot entitled
"Tales of the Unexpected", from December
2008, accompanied a piece by his model
granddaughter Sophie Dahl on the power
and potency of the imagination. Here,
fashion designer Peter Jensen stares with a
mixture of surprise and awkwardness at the
camera while Karen Elson playfully goads
him in floral silk bra and knickers by Agent
Provocateur and Chanel satin shoes.

ANNA CRYER is an editor who has worked
at British *Vogue*, *Tatler* and *Harper's
Bazaar* in London and New York. She was
at *Vogue* on three separate occasions, as
the magazine celebrated its 75th, 90th
and 100th anniversaries. Her childhood
nickname "Pants on Fire" seems prescient
given the subject of this, her first book.
She lives in London.